Through the eyes of ADHD

Bella Rose Rivers

BookLeaf Publishing

India | USA | UK

Presentation by *BookLeaf Publishing*

Web: www.bookleafpub.com

E-mail: info@bookleafpub.com

ISBN: 9789358311327

First edition 2023

This book is dedicated to my family. They have encouraged me to never give up on anything I have wanted to do. My friends have also helped me in this journey by helping me back up whenever I got pushed down.

ACKNOWLEDGEMENT

None of this would be possible without God. He has helped me get through many hardships in my life and has gifted me the talent of writing.

The New Gen

Insecurities are covered with make up.
Feelings are hidden by a smile on your face.
Some kids families think they are a disgrace.

Kids get abused; mentally and physically.
Than those kids have kids, and do the same
thing.
Then the cycle repeats...

The kids of the new gen are than traumatized.
And for that, we can only blame our feelings and
eyes.

We take what has happened to us; and we pass it
down the tree.
Then we expect the next generation to feel
light-weighted and free?

We have to admit it, the world is a cruel and
unforgiving place.
But if we influence the little kids right, they'll
make the world better at their own pace.

Life in 2020

The lost little girl wanted to play. Outside she went day after day. She was happy the sun had started to shine, happy the birds were flying up high.

She ran to a window and called on her friend. But the cat in the window said she couldn't come in.

She noticed a squirrel climbing up a tree and she danced over to him, as happy as can be. "Hi Mr. Squirrel would you be able to play?" But the squirrel shook its head and scampered away. It climbed to the highest part of the tree and jumped to a branch in another canopy.

Determined not to give up, the lost little girl starting acting amuck! She startled a frog who jumped up from the ground, very misplaced as there were no others around. "I'll catch him and then we can go play" but the frog was too quick, it had hopped away.

The lost little girl walked into the clearing. She kept looking around, trying to gather her bearings. The doors were all locked. The windows were closed. The blinds all drawn tight. No cars on the roads.

The lost little girl heaved a big sigh; she sat at the picnic table and started to cry. She waited and hoped for a friend to appear, but after a long while, she slowly disappeared.

- written with my mother.

Expressing Yourself

The way that you express yourself, whether it's clothing or makeup or wealth.

For me, I express myself in art; whether it's a drawing or making a chart.

I like to sketch and dream away. I draw on myself or sketch a bay.

Instead of crying when I'm sad, I sketch and draw and it makes me glad.

In the blink of the eye.

Oh boy, I just turned five! I feel so young and alive. I run and I jump and I play and I tumble. Oh yay, I just turned five.

In the blink of an eye, I am turning sixteen. And today is my sweet sixteen teenage dream!

In the blink of an eye, I'm now graduating from college; 21 and having fun.

In the blink of an eye, now I'm 25. Waking down the aisle. My fiance awaits, and this day is great.

In the blink of an eye, now I'm 36. The time flies so quick and I have two kids.

In the blink of an eye, they just turned five! And today is their party.

In the blink of an eye, they're in grade 5. I have so much time.

In the blink of an eye, how am in 45? I finally decide to start my own business.

In the blink of an eye, I'm a CEO. I have happy days and sad days where I smile or frown.

In the blink of an eye, my kids are graduating from high school. I'm there and I'm proud and we're happy. They look so nice up there on the stands. They're smiling and I'm crying

In the blink of an eye, I'm now 55. My business is doing great. My kids are in college and me and my husband are out of state.

In the blink of an eye, I'm now 65. I have lots of money. My kids are back home. Now I never have to be worried about being alone.

In the blink of an eye, I'm 75. Both my kids have families. My husband likes to live in reality; while I myself, like to live in great fantasies.

In the blink of an eye, I'm now 85. My husband has just died. I'm sobbing and mourning... Now it is the next morning.

In the blink of an eye, I'm now 95. I really have lived, memories help keep me alive.

In the blink of an eye, I'm now one hundred. I
made it.

In the blink of an eye, I have just died. My ghost
walks around saying good-byes. I see the light
come and one last time I mutter to myself;

"In the blink of an eye".

Where I aspire to go

Perfect
Angelic
Romantic
Inspirational
Spectacular

2am

The night time is nice,
Constellations precise.

Stars light up the night,
The moon's very bright.

Everyone is asleep,
So you can't make a peep.

You're up at night,
So you can't use a light.

You fall back asleep,
And in your dreams, you dance and leap.

Mom

Broken toes, bloody nose, microscopic verbal blows.

Narcissisism's in your face, trying hard to escape this fate.

Which ways up? Which ways down? Being made to look the clown.

I can't see. I can't breath. Who do I truly believe?

Plot twist coming. Could it be, that the victim isn't me?

It's my fault. It's all my doing. Poker face is very cunning.

Autoimmunes suck!

She's covered in bruises. She's always fatigued.
She's hardly eats, she can't sleep, and she's
always moody.

She's up early morning, making our world go
smooth. Dogs and cold coffee while making a
lunch or two.

She works all day long, sometimes 2 jobs. It
hurts her to smile. But she manages to do it and I
don't know how.

She shows up to school functions, she shows up
to my games. She takes me to parties and makes
me do my homework (it's such a pain!).

I talk back and I pout and I put on a big show.
She's exhausted and I know it but my antics
make her blow.

What little fight she has left to get through the
day, has just evaporated.

Now we're both done, and I've still got the homework to do. She's trying to make dinner but her eyes keep fighting to stay open.

3 dogs are barking, my sister is tantruming. I'm only 11! None of this should be happening.

I know she cries daily, because she sits in her car. She's home but she's hiding and it kinda hurts my heart.

Oh, here she comes, this place is a zoo! She opens the door and gets knocked through. The dogs are all jumping and Remie is crying.

I stand in the back ground as dad grabs his keys. "Someone needs a ride", but I think he's just escaping. He leaves and she sighs and it's just so chaotic.

We make it through the afternoon and than the evening comes.

My rotten spoiled sister is crying yet again! She only wants "her mommy" and it isn't freaking fair. There's never any time for me. She doesn't ever share. I never get the TV, it's Gabby Cat and Paw Patrol and Frozen or Disney.

What about me? What about meeeeeeee??

Remie finally passes out and Mom gets up for
bed. She stands and struggles to get up the stairs.

I now could watch TV, or play on my phone. It
is almost my bedtime but I need to unwind.

Oh I know.

Up the stairs and into her bed. She's warm and
she's doses off so easily. But I cuddle up and she
pulls me close. She mumbles my speical lullaby.

Love and War

Love and war, like never before. You live and love, like a bird soaring through the sky, such as a dove.

You love and you lose, sometimes it might be abuse. But in all, love is something that will never fall.

Lost Friend

Oh no, I did it again. I messed up and lost a friend. We were doing so well.

What went wrong? Is it something I did or said?

Oh no, I lost a friend again. I guess this is the end.

The glitch in my brain.

The glitch in my brain is hard to relate to, because it is so hard to control.

It makes my emotions go crazy; an emotional roller coster every day.

I go from sad to happy in an instant.

It's like a sickness, except I don't know how to fix it.

Happy to mad to sad, again.

It's like this glitches out roller coaster will never end.

A strong emotion

Aggravating
Narcissism
Guilt
Exasperated
Revenge

My crazy grandma

My grandma is crazy. She likes to drink. One of the things about that is, it makes it so she doesn't think.

She makes everything about her- her life, her problems. She complains and guilt trips, she makes me feel so guilty.

She blurs and she dumps and she empties out her brain. Than she yells at us, like we're the ones to blame!

Yes, I love her, with all of my heart. But she needs to stop drinking and make a band new start.

Masking

Hiding behind a mask, is the truth to much to ask?

We blend with others, even our mothers sometimes don't understand us.

We never open up. We cheer others up, making people laugh.

We change out personality to fit in with people, then we fall.

We sink into a deep pool.

Late

Oh shoot, I'm late! And school starts at eight!
My alarm didn't go off, and I didn't awake.

It's safe to say, I'm going to be late. The teacher
won't understand, and I have to practice with my
band.

I missed my bus now I have to rush! Oh no, I'm
going to be late.

Trap of Life

I'm locked in this room, no light to be seen. My family always punishes me.

No escape from here, I'm trapped here forever.

But when I see my friends, it all gets better!

An escape from it all. I will never fall!

I'll fight it till I reach the end, then I'll be free, never to fall for it again.

Therapy

Don't call me on the phone. Just leave me alone.

I got diagnosed with depression, and the doctor suggested a therapy session.

I sit alone on my phone, at my home. Waiting to go therapy.

The dishes are done, I want to do something fun.

But I have depression, and I need a therapy session.

Friends

Why should I have to apologize, when you can't
see through my eyes.

You can't feel what I feel when you take away
my stuff.

It doesn't help us heal.

No matter what we do, we never fall through.

If we had to pick grades or friends. We would
pick friends, until the very end.

When you take our phones away, we're not like
you. We don't shout "hooray".

When you take away our phones, we can't call or
text our friends or bros.

Just give us a chance to hang out with our
friends.

And maybe you'll see us, when we're not
playing pretend.

ADHD

ADHD makes it hard to do stuff. It's confusing,
chaotic and makes us forget stuff.

If only we could have a chance to show the real
us. You would make us your new friend without
making a fuss.

Little Sister

25

My sister is a crazy kid, she hasn't slept in years.

She cute when she smiles and when she laughs, but then she bursts into tears.

She loves to run, laugh and play, she's loves to dance in the sun.

She's a happy, cheerful, bundle of joy, who loves to have fun.

The Internet

The Internet is bad, but sometimes it's good.
Just a few of it's things are misunderstood.
The videos are good and sometimes there bad.
Most of the statements just make people mad.
It's fine to let your kids watch what they like, but
make sure it's appropriate and polite.